Smitten with Kittens

Ariel Books

Andrews and McMeel
Kansas City

Smitten with
Kittens

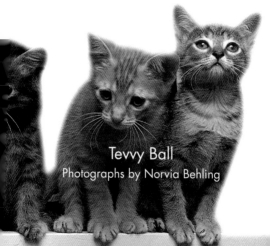

Tevvy Ball

Photographs by Norvia Behling

ISBN: 0-8362-2652-6
Library of Congress Catalog Card Number: 96-85916

Photographs copyright © 1997 by Norvia Behling

Spot art from Art Parts

Book design by Maura Fadden Rosenthal

Contents

Smitten with Kittens

introduction

Kittens, kittens, showers of kittens, visitations of kittens. So many, you see them as Kitten, like leaves growing on a bare branch, staying heavy and green, then falling exactly the same every year. People coming to visit say: What happened to that lovely kitten? What lovely kitten? They are all lovely kittens.

—Doris Lessing

My sister remembers when, as a little girl about nine years old, she was playing in her room one rainy Saturday afternoon and heard a scratching at her window. She looked up, and there was a gray tabby, a tiny kitten gripped in its mouth, pawing at the glass. My sister hurried to open the front door, and the mother cat appeared from the bushes alongside the house, trotted briskly into the front hall, and set the little fellow on the floor. She then headed back into the bushes, from whence she soon emerged with another kitten, followed by another, and then yet another. A few minutes later, the whole family, lacking only a faithless father, was settled on the foyer carpet, with the tender tabby lovingly licking, one by one, each of her wet, squirming brood. My astonished sister, of course, did the only thing she could: She heated up a saucer of milk.

    While kittens captivate us for many reasons, it seems to me that part of their special appeal derives largely from just such occurrences. Puppies are almost always carefully planned purchases; our first encounters with infant felines are frequently suffused with a rather more random joy: The little things have a way of just showing up, catching us with our guard down, and purring their way into our heart.

When my sisters and I were kids, living in what was then relatively rural country north of Los Angeles, it seemed that our rambling frame house was always brightened by at least a couple of rambunctious little fur balls. The names we devised reflected our family's interests; one litter was christened for the knights and ladies of Arthurian legend—Lancelot, Galahad, Guinevere—another for those of Wagnerian myth—Siegfried, Brunhild—while one kitty (a little girl, no less), was, at my insistence, named Koufax. None was ever planned or premeditated, at least not by us; kittens came and went with the ebb and flow of life; we unfailingly took them in, and, when we had to, let them go as well. To paraphrase a famous line about life: Kittens often happen to us while we're busy making other plans.

Cuddly Companions

Of course, there are times when fate fails to provide, and we must seek out the little companion that we have decided, for any of many reasons, we now need. Perhaps our kids require a playmate. Perhaps our cat could use a new friend. Or perhaps we find ourselves craving a cuddly buddy who will keep us company on a lonely winter night, enliven a slow Saturday afternoon, or help ease the tensions after a brutal day at the office. A kitty, we reason, will listen patiently to everything we have to say, responding to our most bitter complaints with a few friendly licks on our face and a playful romp with a ball of yarn. What could be better than that?

A recent survey conducted for the Humane Society suggests that most people acquire their kittens from friends; less than a quarter of America's kitties are obtained through breeders and pet stores. When our house got too full of furry little critters, my parents would decide that the time had come for a little basic sanity to reassert its sovereignty over the household. Indeed,

over the years our family gave away dozens of kittens, to friends and neighbors, baby-sitters and postmen, and milkmen and plumbers—anyone who dared express a hankering for feline companionship. I remember how brokenhearted my sisters and I were the first time we had to part with a litter; my mother, however, eased our grief, gently explaining that we already had several kitties to love, and the new kittens deserved to have a family who could love them with similarly undivided attention.

So one summer afternoon we put Siegfried, Brunhild, and the others into a big grocery box and took them down to

the neighborhood swimming pool. One inquisitive little boy—he must have been about eight—hurried over to find out what this mystery box contained; when he saw the kitties, his eyes opened wide with wonder.

"Can I *touch* them?" he asked.

We allowed that he could.

"Hey, you guys," he then yelled to his friends. "There's a *whole box* of *kittens* over here."

The pool quickly emptied; within a moment or two, perhaps a dozen kids were jostling for position around us. When informed that, if their parents gave the okay, they could take a kitten home, several children made a beeline for their nearby houses. A few returned crestfallen; a few others reappeared triumphant, including the boy who had first checked out the kitty box, who now came running back, shouting to his sister, "They said we could do it."

Joy in Numbers

Yet we need to remember not to allow our fondness for the kitten we may have fallen in love with to obscure the little fellow's own best interests. Kittenhood seems among the most fleeting of nature's gifts, and it's understandable not to want to miss a single day of our kitty's precious youth. However eager we may be to get kitty home, though, we must never separate it from its mother until it is at least eight—and preferably twelve—weeks old. (In the case of a foundling, where you don't have such a choice, you should be sure to provide an extra dose of your own tender loving care.) And with any kitty, when you do bring it home it's important to start cuddling it every day— for most of us, not exactly a painful task.

Some kittens adjust easily, while others take a while to become comfortable in their new surroundings, and you'll want to have a few things on hand in order to facilitate the newcomer's transition into your home. In addition to the obvious items—litter pan and litter, water bowl and food dish, scratching post, grooming tools, some cat food—it's a

good idea to pick up a few safe toys, so that your kitty can start right off with the kinds of activities that come naturally. You'll want to be sure that all toxic h o u s e h o l d materials and all sewing sup-plies—except, perhaps, for a ball of yarn—are safely tucked away, all high windows shut, electric sockets safely covered with socket guards, and so on. And you might get a blanket from kitty's prior living quarters, so that its first days in new surroundings can be softened by the comfort of at least one familiar thing.

It's usually not a good idea, by the way, to rush out and buy an elaborate and expensive cat bed. Kittens are adventurers with minds of their own when it comes to selecting their boudoir, and no cat of mine

has ever actually slept regularly in a bed
I bought for it. They usually seem to opt
for an old armchair, a sofa, a bed, or
the like. And then there was an inquisitive little kitty we named Fiesel; for the
first few weeks after we brought her

home, we never knew where she would stretch out for a catnap, until she discovered the perennial pile of loose laundry on top of the dryer. It was warm, it was soft, and it often purred like mommy. The laundry room became her permanent abode; when we moved into a new house a few years later, after a brief initial period of nervous exploration, Fiesel quickly sought out the dryer and was soon snoozing once more.

If you are bringing a kitten into a household where a mature cat already reigns, the young debutante's coming-out should be handled with appropriate delicacy and social grace. Suggest to your older cat, politely but firmly, that it's time for a brief two-day vacation in the back bedroom. During this time, let the kitten explore undisturbed, so that it can get used to the other cat's scent. You can then put the kitten in a cage and let the older cat come around, sniff a bit, and get used to the intruder. Be sure to lavish loving care on the older cat, so that it doesn't feel left out.

How well the introductions come off will depend on your degree of skill, as well as on your cat's age. If it's younger than five years, things will probably go

smoothly enough. If it's much older, however, it can have difficulty developing a
healthy relationship with a fresh young
upstart. For example, we once brought a
kitten into a household with two cats who

were both over ten years old. The newcomer was never really accepted; the
most cordial arrangement we were able
to procure was a grudging and grumpy
coexistence.

Many people, myself included, sub-
scribe to the theory that when it comes to
kittens, there is definitely joy in numbers.
In other words, if you don't have a cat,
you might consider picking up a couple of
kittens. If you are often away from home,
two kittens of about the same age can
keep each other company. Kittens learn
through play—wrestling, running, jump-
ing, playing with toys—and two can learn

more easily than one. You'll want to be
sure that they get along; the best way to
do this is to take two kitties from the same
litter. They will already have been intro-
duced, and the bond
formed in their
earliest days of
kittenhood

will likely continue to deepen. And you will likely find that the delights of kitten-watching seem to grow in some exponential fashion mysteriously related to how many little fur balls are romping around your living room floor. (Or, as in the case with Siegfried and Brunhild, the dining-room screen door. The kitties would have a race to see who could climb the screen door faster; upon reaching the top, they would both realize that they were stuck and start to howl, at which time one of us would carefully pluck their little claws loose and set them back on the carpet.)

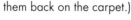

Of course, if your cat has kittens, you will, like it or not (and what's not to like?), find yourself with several handfuls of kittens. This happened to us one Sunday night many years ago, when we came home from a summer weekend excursion to find Fiesel—by then of child-bearing age—ensconced in the large hallway drawer where we kept the bath towels, with five wet little things pressing their faces to her belly. Such an experience opens up one of the great joys of kitten-watching: for a while, these little critters are hopelessly helpless, crawling all over each other in their blind bouts for pre-

ferred feeding stations; then they blossom, almost overnight, into full and frisky kittenhood.

As things turned out, we were perhaps a bit too captivated for Fiesel's taste. A few weeks later, we found the drawer mysteriously bare, and Fiesel, cruelly indifferent to our growing concern, wasn't letting on as to where she had taken her brood. Finally, we were obliged to fall back on a ruse, noisily pretending to go out, then doubling back through the kitchen door in order to spy on our cat. After a few feints—down the hall, up the stairs—to throw off, we

assumed, would-be pursuers, Fiesel sur-
reptitiously made her way to the living
room fireplace, looked around one last
time, and, quick as Saint Nick himself,
leapt up the chimney. When we had
recovered from our surprise, my father
took a flashlight and, rather less gracefully, squeezed his way up into the flue.
They were there, all right, he reported,
six pairs of yellow eyes peering down
from a little ledge just above his head.
After much useless pleading, he was
finally able to reach them and bring them
back down. We thus learned that a
mother cat with little ones needs her

space, which, from then on, we were only too glad to give her.

Purebred Bliss

Should friends and neighbors, as well as inscrutable fate, fail to provide us with the kitty of our dreams, we can always fall back on a pet store or cat breeder. Of course, if you are interested in a purebred kitty, commercial cat suppliers would likely be your first choice. I should perhaps say that, while pedigree has never been a prime concern for me, in certain circles, much is made of such matters. Cats—and, therefore, kittens—do in fact come in more than fifty breeds, and, since the first attempts about one hundred years ago to analyze the differences among them, a number of experts have waxed eloquent over the traits and characteristics of each one. While such splitting of hairs generally pertains more to mature cats than to prancing kittens, it is worth at least brief consideration, because kittenhood is fleeting, and cats, as we all know, are eternal.

According to one such expert, for example, Siamese are "very active" and are the loudest, the most intelligent, and among the most independent-minded of all felines. Oriental shorthairs are also loudmouths, moody, fussy (but then, have you ever met an unfinicky cat?), and demanding of constant attention. At the other end of the scale, Persians are the calmest kitties on the face of the earth, with a soft voice and a loud purr (as kittens, however, they are usually quite playful). Manx, meanwhile, are "some-

what active but quiet"; Cornish Rexes are "people-loving but not napping lap cats"; while American shorthairs are generally quiet, somewhat active, and tend to take life in stride (a few hopeless neurotics aside, what cat doesn't?), except for "a few lines that seem to be timid and easily startled." And so on.

While such comments may often be accurate enough—a friend's Persian, for example, redefines the term "stress-free"—you can get into trouble if you depend on them too much. Another friend has a Siamese who never makes a sound, and who climbs the walls whenever her owner is late arriving home from work—so much for independence. Probably the noisiest cat I have ever heard, for example, is an American shorthair whose early days wandering the Santa Barbara foothills left her with an overriding suspicion of humans with male voices (such as myself) and an incessant need to complain. And while some "experts" may consider Siamese the world's smartest cat, the smartest cat I've ever seen was a mixed-breed tabby, whose intelligence, while perhaps less showy than that of your standard Siamese, was, in my opinion at least, infinitely more idiosyncratic and profound.

Indeed, the vast majority of American cats—some forty million—are nonpedi-greed. They come in all shapes, colors, markings, and shades of personality, and each one,

to hear its owner tell it, is somehow unique. Perhaps it is safest to say that, generally, shorthaired kitties are likely to be active and inquisitive, while longhaired felines tend to appreciate the ample joys of the contemplative life. In fact, though, personality traits are often more a question of nurture than of nature, and unless you're planning a career in the cat-show business, your best bet is to follow your heart. Make sure your little friend is healthy, then be nice, cuddle it often during its formative period (from three to fourteen weeks of age), and you'll probably have a snuggle mate for life.

But when all is said and done, I still maintain that the special magic of kittens comes largely from the fact that they choose us as often as we choose them. Not too long ago, my sister, recently married, was in the process of grilling up some fresh salmon for her first anniversary, when she heard a plaintive meowing coming from the front yard. She opened the door, and there, at the base of the steps, was an emaciated little white Manx who had wandered down from the surrounding hills, lured, no doubt, by the tantalizing fragrance of fresh fish. It stood there trembling, gazing up at my sister with those big kitten eyes, one blue, one green. My sister walked slowly down the stairs, bent over, and put out her two hands in a cupped position; the tiny foundling—wild, shy, shivering—fairly leapt into her palm, and the two have hardly been separated since.

Kitty Quotes

No matter how much cats fight, there always seems to be plenty of kittens.
—Abraham Lincoln

The smallest feline is a masterpiece.
—Leonardo da Vinci

While Alice was sitting curled up in a corner of the great armchair, half talking to herself and half asleep, the kitten had been having a grand game of romps with the ball of worsted Alice had been trying to wind up, and had been rolling it up and down till it had all come undone again; and there it was, spread over the hearthrug, all knots and tangles, with the kitten running after its own tail in the middle.

—Lewis Carroll

Do you see that kitten chasing so prettily her own tail? If you could look with her eyes, you might see her surrounded with hundreds of figures performing complex dramas, with tragic and comic issues, long conversations, many characters, many ups and downs of fate.

—Ralph Waldo Emerson

A kitten is in the animal world what a rosebud is in a garden.
—Robert Southey

If only cats grew into kittens.
—R. D. Stern

Newborn kittens are like blank slates.
—Grace McHattie

A cat with kittens nearly always decides sooner or later to move them.
—Sidney Denham

Two little kittens, one stormy night,
Began to quarrel, and then to fight;
One had a mouse, the other had none,
And that's the way the quarrel begun.
 —Anonymous

Gather kittens while you may,
Time brings only sorrow;
And the kittens of today
Will be old cats tomorrow.
 —Oliver Herford

It is the cry that a cat makes only for her kittens—a soft trilling coo—a pure caress of tone.

    —Lafcadio Hearn

We quickly discovered that two kittens were much more fun than one.
—Allen Lacy

The kitten in the evening pursues his shadow.
—Madame Adele Michelet

Kittens are constantly forgiven.
—Douglas Wilk

The playful kitten with its pretty little tiger-ish gambol is infinitely more amusing than half the people one is obliged to live with in the world.
    —Lady Sydney Morgan

Kittens can happen to anyone.
    —Paul Gallico

No experiment can be more beautiful than that of setting a kitten for the first time before a looking glass.
—Reverend W. Bingley

But buds will be roses,
and kittens, cats,—more's the pity.
—Louisa May Alcott

A kitten is the delight of a household. All day long a comedy is played by this incomparable actor.
—Jules Champfleury

This is the time for you to decide where you want your kitten to sleep. If you let it sleep on your bed the first night it will expect to cuddle up to you for the next eighteen years or so.
—Grace McHattie

See the kitten, how she starts,
Crouches, stretches, paws and darts;
With a tiger-leap half way
Now she meets her coming prey.
Lets it go as fast and then
Has it in her power again.

Now she works with three and four,
Like an Indian conjurer;
Quick as he in feats of art,
Gracefully she plays her part;
Yet were gazing thousands there,
What would little Tabby care?
—William Wordsworth

Another cat? Perhaps. For love there is also a season; its seeds must be resown. But a family cat is not replaceable like a worn-out coat or a set of tires. Each new kitten becomes its own cat, and none is repeated. I am four cats old, measuring out my life in friends that have succeeded but not replaced one another.

—Irving Townsend

...the daintiest little kitten imaginable. It was just like a swansdown powder puff.
—Théophile Gautier

They say the test of literary power is whether a man can write an inscription. I say, "Can he name a kitten?"
—Samuel Butler

. . . A pretty playful kitten . . . is now pert and roguish, now timid and demure, according to its own sweet will.

—Anne Brontë

As one who has long been a pushover for cats, I should like to offer a packet of colorfast, preshrunk advice: If a stray kitten bounds out of nowhere when you're taking a walk, mews piteously, and rubs a soft shoulder against your leg, flee to the hills until the danger is over.

—Murray Robinson

The kitten was six weeks old. It was enchanting, a delicate fairy-tale cat. . . . From the front, sitting with her slender paws straight, she was an exotically beautiful beast. She sat, a tiny thing, in the middle of a yellow carpet, surrounded by five worshipers, not at all afraid of us. Then she stalked around that floor of the house, inspecting every inch of it, climbed up onto my bed, crept under the fold of a sheet, and was at home.

—Doris Lessing

A kitten is so flexible that she is almost double; the hind parts are equivalent to another kitten with which the forepart plays. She does not discover that her tail belongs to her until you tread on it.
    —Henry David Thoreau

Kittenhood, the baby time . . . of cats, is with most the brightest, sprightliest, and prettiest period of their existence, and perhaps the most happy.
    —Harrison Weir

A child is a person who can't understand why someone would give away a perfectly good kitten.
—Doug Larson

Nothing is more playful than a young cat.
   —Thomas Fuller

There is no more intrepid explorer than a kitten.
   —Jules Champfleury

It is a very inconvenient habit of kittens (Alice had once made the remark) that whatever you say to them, they *always* purr.
—Lewis Carroll

An ordinary kitten will ask more questions than any five-year-old.
—Carl Van Vechten

Confront a child, a puppy, and a kitten with sudden danger; the child will turn instinctively for assistance, the puppy will grovel in abject submission to the impending visitation, the kitten will brace its tiny body for a frantic resistance.

—Saki

...Those dear, sweet little lumps, stumping, and padding about the house, pulling over electric lamps, making little puddles in slippers, crawling up my legs, onto my lap (my legs are scratched by them, like Lazarus's), I see myself finding a kitten in the sleeve when I'm putting on my coat, and my tie under the bed when I want to put it on. . . .

—Karel Capek

A kitten is chiefly remarkable for rushing
about like mad at nothing whatever, and
generally stopping before it gets there.
—Agnes Repplier